First World War
and Army of Occupation
War Diary
France, Belgium and Germany

32 DIVISION
Divisional Troops
Divisional Cyclist Company
10 August 1915 - 31 May 1916

WO95/2380/2

The Naval & Military Press Ltd
www.nmarchive.com
Published in association with The National Archives

Published by

The Naval & Military Press Ltd

Unit 10 Ridgewood Industrial Park,

Uckfield, East Sussex,

TN22 5QE England

Tel: +44 (0) 1825 749494

www.naval-military-press.com

www.nmarchive.com

This diary has been reprinted in facsimile from the original. Any imperfections are inevitably reproduced and the quality may fall short of modern type and cartographic standards.

© **Crown Copyright**
Images reproduced by permission of The National Archives, London, England, 2015.

Contents

Document type	Place/Title	Date From	Date To
Heading	WO95/2380 (2)		
Heading	32nd Division Divl Troops Divl Cyclist Coy. Nov 1915-May 1916		
Heading	32nd Divl. Cycl. Coy. Vol V Nov 15		
War Diary	Wensley Yorkshire	10/08/1915	24/08/1915
War Diary	Leodford Wiltshire	21/11/1915	21/11/1915
War Diary	Southampton	21/11/1915	21/11/1915
War Diary	Havre	22/11/1915	22/11/1915
War Diary	Pont Remy	23/11/1915	23/11/1915
War Diary	Francieres	23/11/1915	28/11/1915
War Diary	Flesselles	28/11/1915	28/11/1915
Heading	32nd Divl L. Cycl Coy Vol 2 121/7928		
War Diary	Flesselles.	11/12/1915	11/12/1915
War Diary	Beaucourt	11/12/1915	14/12/1915
War Diary	Baizieux	14/12/1915	15/12/1915
Heading	32nd Divisional Troops 32nd Divisional Cyclist Company January 1916		
War Diary	Baizieux	02/01/1916	02/01/1916
War Diary	Senlis	02/01/1916	30/01/1916
Heading	32nd Divisional Troops 32nd Divisional Cyclist Company February 1916		
War Diary	Senlis	03/02/1916	13/02/1916
War Diary	Henencourt	13/02/1916	13/02/1916
War Diary	Senlis	13/02/1916	13/02/1916
War Diary	Henencourt	18/02/1916	29/02/1916
Heading	32nd Divisional Troops 32nd Divisional Cyclist Company March 1916		
War Diary	Henencourt	01/03/1916	21/03/1916
War Diary	Millencourt	26/03/1916	26/03/1916
War Diary	Henencourt	27/03/1916	31/03/1916
Heading	32nd Divisional Troops 32nd Divisional Cyclist Company April 1916		
War Diary	Henencourt	01/04/1916	03/04/1916
War Diary	Senlis	03/04/1916	30/04/1916
War Diary	Henencourt	23/02/1916	23/02/1916
War Diary	Senlis	09/04/1916	09/04/1916
Heading	32nd Divisional Troops Became "A" Company Xth Corps Cyclist Battalion 31.5.16 32nd DivisionaL Cyclist Company May 1916		
War Diary	Senlis	02/05/1916	31/05/1916

west / 2380 (2)

west / 2380 (2)

32ND DIVISION
DIVL TROOPS

DIVL CYCLIST COY.
NOV 1915 - MAY 1916

32ND DIVISION
DIVL TROOPS

1794/121

32nd Brit. Gds. Bz.
Pol II

Nov 15
/
may 16

Army Form C. 2118

WAR DIARY
or
INTELLIGENCE SUMMARY
32nd Divisional Cyclist Company.
(Erase heading not required.)

Instructions regarding War Diaries and Intelligence Summaries are contained in F.S. Regs, Part II. and the Staff Manual respectively. Title Pages will be prepared in manuscript.

Place	Date	Hour	Summary of Events and Information	Remarks and references to Appendices
Wensley, Yorkshire	10/8/15	—	Company formed. The company was made up from men of the various battalions in the 32nd Division.	
-do-	24/8/15	—	Moved from Wensley to Codford (Wilts).	
Codford, Wiltshire	21/11/15	1.5 pm	Proceeded to Southampton en route for France.	
Southampton	21/11/15	6.30 pm	Crossed to Havre (France)	
Havre	22/11/15	10 am	Disembarked & proceeded to Rest Camp.	
-do-	22/11/15	11 pm	Proceeded by rail to Pont Remy.	
Pont Remy	23/11/15	2 pm	Marched to Lanvières.	
Lanvières	23/11/15	4 pm	Billeted in Lanvières.	
-do-	28/11/15	9 am	Marched to Flesselles.	
Flesselles	28/11/15	4 pm	Billeted in Flesselles.	

M.A. Walton Lieut
for 32nd Divisional Cyclist Company.

32nd Div: L: Cycl. Coy.
Vol: 2

121/7928

Army Form C. 2118

WAR DIARY
32nd Divisional Cyclist Company.
INTELLIGENCE SUMMARY

(Erase heading not required.)

Instructions regarding War Diaries and Intelligence Summaries are contained in F. S. Regs., Part II. and the Staff Manual respectively. Title Pages will be prepared in manuscript.

Place	Date	Hour	Summary of Events and Information	Remarks and references to Appendices
Hesdeville	11/12/15	10.15am	Marched to Beaucourt.	nm
Beaucourt	11/12/15	11.35am	Billeted in Beaucourt.	nm
Beaucourt	14/12/15	6.30pm	Marched to Baizieux.	nm
Baizieux	14/12/15	8.0pm	Billeted in Baizieux.	nm
Baizieux	15/12/15		Company Employed as Working Parties and Cyclist Orderlies to Division and Brigade Headquarters.	nm

MacMillan Lieut
for O.C. 32nd Divisional Cyclist Coy.

32nd Divisional Troops

32nd DIVISIONAL CYCLIST COMPANY

JANUARY 1 9 1 6

WAR DIARY
or
INTELLIGENCE SUMMARY
(Erase heading not required.)

Army Form C. 2118

Instructions regarding War Diaries and Intelligence Summaries are contained in F.S. Regs., Part II. and the Staff Manual respectively. Title Pages will be prepared in manuscript.

Place	Date	Hour	Summary of Events and Information	Remarks and references to Appendices
Bergueux.	2/1/16	12 noon	Marched to Senlis.	"""
Senlis.	2/1/16	1 p.m.	Billeted in Senlis.	"""
Senlis.	3/1/16	—	Company employed as working parties and cyclist orderlies to Division and Brigade Headquarters.	"""
Senlis.	23/1/16	—	Instructions received to reconnoitre the ANCRE valley between AUTHUILLE and The Mill R.24.a.6/3.	"""
Senlis.	25/1/16	—	Reconnaissance commenced. One Officer and 6 other ranks proceeded daily to the valley until the Reconnaissance completed on 28/1/16.	"""
Senlis.	29/1/16	6.15 p.m.	Instructions received to furnish a standing patrol of 1 Officer and 25 other ranks at Eastern end of bridge at Q.50.a.5.9. to watch the ANCRE valley on nights 29/30 Jan. Above party left Senlis at 7.30 p.m. on 29th, and returned at noon 30th Jan. safely.	"""
Senlis.	30/1/16	9.30 a.m.	Instructions received to furnish a standing patrol of 1 Officer on N.C.O. and 10 men nightly at place above mentioned, instead of 25 other ranks.	"""

[signature] W.H. Hunt

33rd Divisional Cyclist Company.

32nd Divisional Troops

32nd DIVISIONAL CYCLIST COMPANY

FEBRUARY 1 9 1 6

WAR DIARY
INTELLIGENCE SUMMARY

(Erase heading not required.)

Army Form C. 2118

Instructions regarding War Diaries and Intelligence Summaries are contained in F.S. Regs., Part II. and the Staff Manual respectively. Title Pages will be prepared in manuscript.

Place	Date	Hour	Summary of Events and Information	Remarks and references to Appendices
SENLIS.	5/2/16	5 pm.	Working party of 12 N.C.Os. + men under the command of an Officer proceed to ANCRE valley to construct Breastworks during the hours of darkness, as cover for standing patrol. The party to proceed each night until the work is completed.	"""
SENLIS.	13/2/16	11 am.	moved to HENENCOURT.	"""
HENENCOURT	13/2/16	noon.	Billeted.	"""
SENLIS.	13/2/16	noon.	Duties in ANCRE valley handed over to H.Q. 4 9th Division.	"""
HENENCOURT.	18/2/16	—	Instructions received to hold two platoons in readiness to proceed as rapidly as possible to the grenade store, AVELUY CRUCIFIX CORNER, in case of a hostile attack at any time. These platoons to be used to insert detonators in the grenades and to issue them to the battalions of the Divisional Reserve, on arrival of the latter. Immediate steps taken to train every man of the company in detonating of bombs.	"""
"	19/2/16	—	Nothing to report.	"""
"	20/2/16 to 28/2/16	—		"""
"	29/2/16	—	Up to this date, the above mentioned two platoons have not been called out for detonating of Hand Grenades. At this date, 35 N.C.Os. + men have gone through a full course of Bomb Throwing & handling, and	""" Lieut., """
"	29/2/16	—	130 N.C.Os. + men have been trained in detonating of grenades.	"""

O.C. 32nd Divisional Cyclist Company.

32nd Divisional Troops

32nd DIVISIONAL CYCLIST COMPANY

MARCH 1 9 1 6

Army Form C. 2118

WAR DIARY
INTELLIGENCE SUMMARY
(Erase heading not required.)

32nd Divisional Cyclist Company
March 1916.

Instructions regarding War Diaries and Intelligence Summaries are contained in F.S. Regs., Part II. and the Staff Manual respectively. Title Pages will be prepared in manuscript.

Place	Date	Hour	Summary of Events and Information	Remarks and references to Appendices
HENENCOURT.	1/3/16	—	Company employed as Working Parties and Cyclist Orderlies to Division & Brigade Headquarters.	Sd.
-do-	1/3/16 to 19/3/16	—	Nothing to report.	Sd.
-do-	19/3/16	—	G.O.C., 32nd Division directs that the Divisional mounted troops carry out training in open warfare & musketry. For this purpose, all working parties & employed men of this company will be placed at the disposal of the C.O. on Tuesday & Friday of each week until further notice.	Sd.
-do-	21/3/16	9 a.m.	Training commenced as above.	Sd.
MILLENCOURT.	26/3/16	7.45pm	76 N.C.Os. & men under the command of Lieut. F. J. Walker carried out practice Bombing attack similar to that carried out by 1st Batt. Dorset Regt. on the preceding evening, whilst the latter unit proceeded to the trenches to carry out the actual attack. As this practice had taken place each night in view of the German trenches, it was considered necessary to continue same this evening to avoid attracting undue notice.	Sd.
HENENCOURT.	27/3/16 to 31/3/16	—	Nothing to report.	Sd.

McSwan [?]
O. C.
32nd Divisional Cyclist Company.

32nd Divisional Troops

32nd DIVISIONAL CYCLIST COMPANY

APRIL 1916

Army Form C. 2118

32nd Divisional Cyclist Company.
April 1916

WAR DIARY
INTELLIGENCE SUMMARY
(Erase heading not required.)

Instructions regarding War Diaries and Intelligence Summaries are contained in F.S. Regs., Part II. and the Staff Manual respectively. Title Pages will be prepared in manuscript.

Place	Date	Hour	Summary of Events and Information	Remarks and references to Appendices
HENENCOURT.	1/4/16	—	Company employed in Working Parties and Cyclist Orderlies to Division or Brigade Headquarters.	
HENENCOURT.	3/4/16	11 am	Moved to SENLIS.	
SENLIS.	3/4/16	noon	Billeted	
-do-	9/4/16	—	Captain G.K. OLIVER. (The Queens Regt.) from 7th Divisional Cyclist Company, takes over command of the company vice Captain H.B. COBB struck off the strength 9/3/16. (authority War Office letter (A.G.4.b.5) dated 9/3/16.)	
-do-	16/4/16	—	2/LIEUT. G.E. JOHNSON slightly wounded (accidentally) in the heck with a faulty Grenade.	
-do-	19/4/16	—	2/LIEUT. G.E. JOHNSON rejoined the Company for duty	
-do-	26/4/16	—	2/LIEUT. A. GIBBONS. from Base Depot. Taken on the strength of the Company from this date.	
-do-	27/4/16 to 30/4/16	—	nothing to report.	

G.K. Oliver
Captain
O.C 32nd Divisional Cyclist Company.

Army Form C. 2118

WAR DIARY
or
INTELLIGENCE SUMMARY
(Erase heading not required.)

32nd Divisional Cyclist Company.

Supplement to April 1916.

Place	Date	Hour	Summary of Events and Information	Remarks and references to Appendices
HENENCOURT	23/2/16		Captain H.E. Cobb. having been granted extension of leave in United Kingdom by Indian Base, Lieut J.M.A. Hamilton assumes Command of this Company.	S.H.O.
SENLIS	4/April/16		Lieut M.A. Hamilton relinquishes Command of the Company on arrival of Captain G.W. Oliver, (The Queen's Regt).	S.H.O.

G.W. Oliver
Captain
Comdg: 32nd Divisional Cyclist Coy.

32nd Divisional Troops

Became "A" Company Xth Corps Cyclist Battalion

31.5.16.

32nd DIVISIONAL CYCLIST COMPANY

M A Y 1 9 1 6

32 Div Cyclists

WAR DIARY
~~INTELLIGENCE SUMMARY~~
(Erase heading not required.)

Army Form C. 2118

32nd Divisional Cyclist Company.

May 1916

Place	Date	Hour	Summary of Events and Information	Remarks and references to Appendices
SENLIS.	2/5/16.	11-30am.	One Platoon sent to reconnoitre the tracks in the Divisional Area. Every man fully acquainted with all places of importance in the track. The section of above Platoon was shelled by a shell and sustained the following casualties. 6 Killed. O.R. 2. Died of wounds. O.R. 1. Wounded. O.R. 2.	Killed 9316 Pte Grant. P.M. 10340 Sgreen J. Died of Wounds 10171 Pte Scott. W. Wounded 10344 L/Cpl Hargo M. 10338 Pte Donnelly B.
SENLIS	3/5/16 to 9/5/16.	—	Company engaged in training & also taken part in Divisional training in the attack. In this training one Platoon of the Coy is attached to each time mentioned Battery in the Division, for the purpose of carrying ammunition. This training is carried out over an area marked to represent the actual line here, in the Divisional Area.	500
SENLIS.	9/5/16 to 16/5/16.	—	Company in training.	
SENLIS.	17/5/16 to 30/5/16	—	Company engaged in work with Divisional Signal Company, digging a trench for laying cables.	500
SENLIS.	31/5/16	—	The undermentioned transfers take place, in formation of Cyclist Coys into Corps Cyclist Battalion. This Company now becomes "A" Company X Corps Cyclist Battalion. Lieut Hamilton M.R., Lieut J.A. Bare, 2/Lieut P.A. Gibbons, and 9 O.R. transferred to No. 3 Base Depot. 93 O.Rs. are transferred to 19th Bn. Lancashire Fusiliers. 6 O.Rs. are transferred to Hd. Qrs. X Corps Cyclist Bn.	500

S.T. Oliver — Captain
Comdg. 32nd Divisional Cyclist Coy.

www.ingramcontent.com/pod-product-compliance
Lightning Source LLC
Chambersburg PA
CBHW081510160426
43193CB00014B/2638